CHRISTIAN CLA

MW01004678

THE WESLEYS

Amazing Love

6 studies
for individuals
or groups
with study notes

CLASSICS

Carolyn Nystrom

CAROLYN NYSTROM, Series Editor

InterVarsity Press
Downers Grove, Illinois

InterVarsity Press
P.O. Box 1400, Downers Grove, IL 60515-1426
World Wide Web: www.ivpress.com
E-mail: mail@ivpress.com

*InterVarsity Press® is the book-publishing division of InterVarsity Christian Fellowship/USA®,
a student movement active on campus at hundreds of universities, colleges and schools of
nursing in the United States of America, and a member movement of the International
Fellowship of Evangelical Students. For information about local and regional activities, write
Public Relations Dept., InterVarsity Christian Fellowship/USA, 6400 Schroeder Rd., P.O. Box
7895, Madison, WI 53707-7895, or visit the IVCF website at <www.ivcf.org>.*

*All Scripture quotations, unless otherwise indicated, are taken from the Holy Bible, New
International Version®. NIV®. Copyright ©1973, 1978, 1984 by International Bible Society.
Used by permission of Zondervan Publishing House. All rights reserved.*

The chart entitled "The Wesley Family Tree" in the introduction is taken from Susanna, Mother
of the Wesleys *by Rebecca Lamar Harmon ©1968 by Abingdon Press. Used by permission.*

The excerpt in study one is taken from The Works of John Wesley, *ed by W. Reginald Ward and
Richard P. Heizenrater ©1988 by Abingdon Press. Used by permission.*

The excerpt in study three is taken from The New Birth *by Thomas C. Oden ©1984 by Thomas
C. Oden. Reprinted by permission of HarperCollins Publishers, Inc.*

Cover and interior illustrations: Roberta Polfus

ISBN 0-8308-2087-6

Printed in the United States of America ∞

P	18	17	16	15	14	13	12	11	10	9	8	7	6	5	4	3	2	1
Y	16	15	14	13	12	11	10	09	08	07	06	05	04	03	02			

CONTENTS

Introducing
The Wesleys

God has threaded the influence of John and Charles Wesley through my life—though often I didn't notice the weavings. It began with my conversion when I was nine years old. In a holiness church in rural southern Ohio, I walked the aisle and (in typical Wesleyan fashion) knelt at the mourner's bench. There I cried—not much; I wasn't the emotional sort even then. But at the mourner's bench I wept a tear or two over my sin and the marvel of Jesus' love for me. No one said the name Wesley that night; the emphasis was on Jesus—a fact that would have pleased the Wesleys. But American revivalism (and my redemption) is a heritage from the Wesleys, even though they spent a bare two years on our soil.

My growing up years saw my family crossing a great theological divide—from holiness to Reformed. I had no idea we were crossing a chasm two hundred years deep. We simply changed churches. But I have been some version of Reformed ever since—Reformed with a twist, however. I have a deep and lasting respect for Wesleyan faith and for Wesleyan practice of that faith. So what's a Presbyterian elder doing writing a foreword about the Wesleys? Expressing her thanks.

My appreciation for the Wesleys got a fresh boost when I met a young man who later became my son-in-law. Joel came from generations of Methodist pastors, missionaries and seminary teachers. I saw that these people loved Jesus and they delighted in his love for them. They practiced the daily disciplines of holy living, not because they were afraid of God's wrath, but because they wanted to please the God they loved. Their hearts were as warm as their laughter. They were like the aroma of apple blossoms wafting through the steel-bound intellectual rigors of my own spiritual heritage. They reminded me of my first spiritual home.

Later I visited friends who lived on St. Simons Island, Georgia. They took me to Epworth, where John Wesley lived and preached and suffered spiritual torment from 1735 to 1737. Even the names on St. Simons Island (Epworth and Christ's Church) speak of Wesley's home in England. I walked the island in humid July heat, twined my fingers through Spanish moss draping ancient live oak trees, stood in the tiny white chapel where Wesley prayed and looked out over the ocean where he longed for home. And I wondered at the power of God, who used two of John Wesley's most stumbling years to spread his influence over a continent. As John Wesley headed for home in emotional turmoil and spiritual defeat, he could not know that within eighty years the nation at his back would house some two thousand Methodist churches.

A retreat on spiritual formation brought me once again to the Wesleys. Richard Foster, in explaining how he formed his pattern for Renovaré, spoke of John Wesley's "classes." These classes were not people dressed in Sunday finery sitting in rows for lecture and laughter. Wesley's classes were men and women gathered in homes at midweek to examine their souls. Sample questions John Wesley asked of himself include: "Have I thought anything too dear to part with, to serve my neighbor? Have I in speaking to a stranger explained what religion is not? And what it is? Have I thought or spoken unkindly of [my neighbor]? Have I duly used intercession . . . for my friends on Sunday? For my pupils on Monday? For the family in which I am every day?" These spiritually courageous men and women asked and answered similar questions of each other. They grew sturdy in the practice of their faith. After the retreat I created my own patterns (methods) of prayer, a practice that continued for years. If John Wesley glanced at my prayer book, he would recognize his own fingerprints.

I am not a Wesleyan; I have crossed the theological chasm to the "other camp." But Christ himself bridges that gulf. And so I invite all to sing Charles Wesley and be refreshed, to read John Wesley and be filled.

The Wesley Era

"A brand plucked out of the burning," said Samuel as he sheltered his five-year-old son in his arms and watched his rectory crumble in flames. It was a description his son claimed all of his life. The large family had been asleep when the fire began (possibly started by a disgruntled parishioner). Hetty, age eleven, had woken first when she was nearly hit by a piece of burning thatch. She shouted an alarm, and the parents and the family nurse grabbed the children and ran. No one noticed that one still slept in the bed he shared with two sisters. Finally awake, he stood at the second floor window. Neighbors ran for a ladder while his father charged at the stairs. Flames drove back the pastor, and there was no time for a ladder. One neighbor hoisted another to his shoulders. The top man stretched, lunged and grabbed the boy. The house collapsed on itself. John Wesley would live.

Eight million United Methodists can thank God. So can a large assortment of Wesleyans, Free Methodists, Nazarenes, members of the Salvation Army (and those they serve), African Methodist Episcopals, people of the AME Zion tradition, along with a host of Pentecostals and charismatics. John Wesley was their founder. But those not part of the Wesley tradition also receive God's blessing through his life. As we serve our neighbors, love our Lord and try daily to express that love through our actions and our worship, we gain support from the life and writings of the Wesleys.

The chart on page 8 summarizes the Wesley family members. Susanna was born in 1669, John in 1703 and Charles in 1707.

The Wesley Family Tree
The Epworth Wesley Family[1]

Name	Birthplace	Born	Died	Burial Place	Age
Samuel Wesley, Sr.[2]	Whitchurch	late in 1662	4/25/1735	Epworth Churchyard	73
Susanna	London	1/20/1669	7/23/1742	Bunhill Fields, London	73
Children					
1. Samuel Jr.	London	2/10/1690	11/6/1739	Tiverton	49
2. Susanna	South Ormsby	1691	4/1693	South Ormsby	Infant
3. Emilia (Harper)	South Ormsby	1/1692	1771	London	79
4. Annesley 5. Jedediah twins	South Ormsby	1694	1/31/1695	South Ormsby	Infants
6. Susanna (Ellison)	South Ormsby	1695	12/7/1764	London	69
7. Mary (Whitelamb)[3]	South Ormsby	1696	11/1734	Wroote	38
8. Mehetabel (Wright)	Epworth	1697	3/21/1750	London	53
9. Not known whether boy or girl	Epworth	1698	soon died	Epworth	Infant
10. John	Epworth	5/18/1699	soon died	Epworth	Infant
11. Benjamin	Epworth	1700	soon died	Epworth	Infant
12. & 13. Unnamed twins	Epworth	5/17/1701	soon died	Epworth	Infant
14. Anne (Lambert)	Epworth	1702	?		
15. John	Epworth	6/17/1703	3/2/1791	City Road, London	87
16. Son smothered by nurse	Epworth	5/8/05	5/30/05	Epworth	Infant
17. Martha (Hall)	Epworth	5/8/1706	7/19/1791	City Road, London	85
18. Charles	Epworth	12/18/1707	3/29/1788	Marylebone, London	80
19. Kezziah	Epworth	3/1709	3/9/1741	London	32

Chart taken from *Susanna, Mother of the Wesleys* by Rebecca Lamar Harmon. ©1968 by Abingdon Press. Used by permission.

---

[1] Data assembled chiefly from Stevenson's *Memorials of the Wesley Family* and Adam Clarke's *Memoirs of the Wesley Family*.
[2] Stevenson gives 12/17/1662 as Samuel Wesley's birth date, but Kirk, the parish register of Whitchurch, gives 12/17/1662 as the date of his baptism.
[3] Stevenson lists Mary Wesley's place of birth as Epworth in 1696, but Dr. Frank Baker's more recent research establishes 1697 as the date of arrival of the Wesley's at Epworth, so Mary must have been born at South Ormsby.

John Wesley would have been surprised at his denominational progeny. He was an Anglican, a member of the Church of England, and remained so all of his life. He took communion every week, even though his critics thought that practice "popish." Beginning with his student days at Oxford, Wesley formed "Holy Clubs" (later termed societies or classes), where small groups of people gathered to support each other in holy living and spiritual growth. Even though he ordained preachers (when the Church of England would not), Wesley never thought of these groups as a separate denomination. In his mind they were societies within the mother church. Even today, if we move from an Episcopal worship service to a Methodist meeting, once we get below the surface of stained glass, preferred music and liturgical form, we find much in common. In this, at least, Wesley would be pleased.

Early Years

John and Charles Wesley were born to Samuel Wesley and Susanna Annesley Wesley. The brothers were among the nineteen children born to this marriage. We can wonder at Susanna's stamina (and well we should), but she herself was the youngest of twenty-five! Susanna was sturdy in spirit as well as body. On one occasion she refused to echo an "amen" to her husband's prayer. (He was praying for King William, a political opponent to her favorite, the exiled King James II.) Samuel became so angry that he refused to live with her for six months.

Susanna educated each of her children. She began by forbidding them to read until their fifth birthday. At that point she taught them the alphabet and began their reading instruction with the first chapters of Genesis. She held classes for six hours each day and reserved evenings for spiritual instruction—which she gave to each child one-on-one. John's letters to her throughout his formal schooling show that he continued to feel comfortable talking with her about the welfare of his soul and that, in many ways, she was his theological peer.

Samuel's high moral standards and unpopular political beliefs angered many people, including those in his own parish. People in his area did not express their disagreement kindly. They crippled his cows and at one point had him thrown into prison for not being able to pay a debt on immediate demand. During his short stay in prison John's father passed out books, began worship services and declared that he was "getting acquainted with my brother jailbirds as fast as I can." Later John also took up prison ministry. He visited prisoners, taught them to read, provided free medical care and created Wesley's Benevolent Loan Fund to help them finance new businesses.

At School

Both John and Charles received a classical education usually reserved for the rich—which they were not. Wealthy friends and political leaders, along with their older brother Samuel, made the necessary arrangements. They studied at Oxford where teachers complained that John did his assignments but wasted his time in wide reading that "did little except feed his intellectual curiosity." He came away with a love for literature, which he could read in six languages including, of course, the ancient biblical languages of Greek and Hebrew. Soon after he had officially finished school, John's wide readings took him to *Imitation of Christ* by Thomas à Kempis, *Rule and Exercises of Holy Living and Dying* by Bishop Jeremy Taylor, and *Christian Perfection* and *Serious Call* by William Law. John considered these men of faith his spiritual fathers. Throughout his life their writings are echoed in his own.

John was also interested in medicine. Once while at Oxford he got a severe nosebleed that he could not stop by ordinary means. So he stripped and jumped into the cold river. The bleeding stopped, as he cheerfully reported in a letter to his mother. He also followed his father's recommendation to run, each morning, three times around the school property—a sight that must have seemed as odd as the spiritual intensity of his Holy Club. Eventually (in 1778), he wrote a medical book, *Primitive Physic*. The book went through nearly a hundred editions. Though medical experts declared it full of superstition, people who followed it probably came to less harm than those who endured the standard medical practices of that day.

The Methodists

From his early days at Oxford, John was distressed by the lack of spiritual fervor among his fellow classmates and later his colleagues. Declaring, "There is no such thing as a solitary Christian," the Wesley brothers began a Holy Club. Members of this group met regularly for prayer and personal accountability. They agreed to fast twice a week, examine themselves regularly for sin, participate in the regular liturgies of the church, pray several times a day and perform acts of service for the needy. This pattern of spiritual accountability within a small group became a lifelong pattern of Wesleyan ministry. But at Oxford this patterned form of spirituality did not meet with respect. By 1735 participants in the Holy Club were unkindly dubbed "methodists."

Yet the Wesleys accepted the name—and redefined it. Spiritual method, according to John Wesley, was full of joyful abandon in love for God. In "A Plain Account of Christian Perfection" (1753), John Wesley wrote, "A *Methodist* is one who loves the Lord his God with all his heart, with all his soul, with all his mind, and with all his strength. God is the joy of his heart and the desire of his soul which is continually crying out, *Whom have I in Heaven but you; and there is none upon earth whom I desire besides you. My God and my all! You are the strength of my heart, and my portion forever.* He is therefore happy in God, yea always happy, as having in him a well of water springing up into everlasting life, and overflowing his soul with peace and joy."

To America

In 1735 John and Charles Wesley sailed to Georgia with the hope of serving as missionaries to the Indians as well as strengthening the church among the settlers there. The work did not go well. Local people considered Wesleyan religion far too strenuous, and John had an unhappy affair of the heart with Miss Sophia Hopkey. John left after a mere two years. But one event influenced the Wesley brothers as much as any other thus far. They met the Moravians. Twenty-six German emigrants traveled on the same ship. Their songs, full of meaning and worship, inspired Charles to create Christian hymns beyond any the world had known at that point. (He wrote more than six thousand.) The Moravians also prompted John to search for deeper faith. (They sang during a storm while he shivered with fear of death.) John later insisted that he was not truly redeemed until two years later when his heart was "strangely warmed," and he was filled with a full assurance of his own salvation. Indeed, from that point on, John's journals and sermons are full of a love for Jesus and a confidence in Christ's love for him. It seems that God began to answer John's prayer poem written in 1738 on the ship returning from Georgia:

> O grant that nothing in my soul
>   May dwell, but thy *pure love alone!*
> O may thy love *possess me whole,*
>   My joy, my treasure, and my crown;
> Strange fires far from my heart remove:
> My *every act, word, thought, be love!*

Preaching Patterns

Because he was not well accepted by established churches and because his greatest desire was to reach people who were not in church (or whom the church would not accept), John preached mostly outdoors. His routine was to get up at 4:00 a.m., preach his first sermon by 5:00, then preach two or three more in the same day. His preaching style was not loud ranting (which was common in his day), but reasoned and thoughtful—inviting all who listened to abandon their sins and to follow Christ. He traveled on horseback some sixty miles a day in all kinds of weather. He slept wherever he was offered space, sometimes in a cellar, sometimes outdoors, where he might have to shake the ice out of his hair when he woke up. Still he preached (and sang) the love of God. Thousands of oppressed people, who believed that no one loved them, heard and accepted love from God.

The Wesley Legacy

It is hard to overstate the contribution of John and Charles Wesley to the Christian faith. Charles Wesley's hymns still fill our churches today. Not limited to his own company, they are as likely to be sung by Lutherans, Episcopalians, Baptists, Presbyterians, even Moravians, in every corner of the world where God's people worship the risen Lord.

John Wesley's writings fill some forty volumes—enough to make a poor man rich. Yet he limited himself to thirty pounds a year for personal expenses and declared that at his death (whenever that might come) his estate should consist of no more than ten pounds. Six of these pounds would go to hire six men, who needed work, to carry his plain wood casket. With this financial plan he was able to give away, in his lifetime, royalty income of forty thousand pounds. Friends carried out his wishes at his death. He died at the age of eighty-eight, calm and full of faith with the final words, "The best of all is, God is with us."

How to Use a Christian Classics Bible Study

Christian Classics Bible studies are designed to introduce some of the key writers, preachers and teachers who have shaped our Christian thought over the centuries. Each guide has an introduction to the life and thought of a particular writer and six study sessions. The studies each have an introduction to the particular themes and writings in that study and the following components.

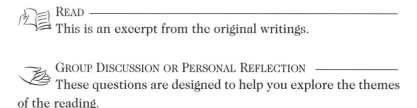

READ ─────────────────────────────────
This is an excerpt from the original writings.

GROUP DISCUSSION OR PERSONAL REFLECTION ──────────
These questions are designed to help you explore the themes of the reading.

INTO THE WORD ————————————————————————

This includes a key Scripture to read and explore inductively. The text picks up on the themes of the study session.

ALONG THE ROAD ————————————————————————

These are ideas to carry you further and deeper into the themes of the study. Some can be used in a group session; many are for personal use and reflection.

The study notes at the end of the guide offer further helps and background on the study questions.

May these writings and studies enrich your life in Christ.

I
ENCOURAGING LOVE
Matthew 14:22-36

*H*ave you ever thought for a moment that maybe you were about to die? A truck headed straight at you in the passing lane? A near drowning? Or maybe that sudden start when you wake from a dream that has you falling, falling, falling? Once that moment passed (and you survived), what did you discover about your thoughts of life—and death?

John Wesley had the opportunity to make that kind of self-observation. In October of 1735 he sailed from England with three other members of the Oxford Club to do mission work for the Indians and colonists at St. Simon's Island off the coast of Georgia. His small party included his brother Charles, as well as Charles Delamot and Ben Ingram. (They planned that George Whitefield would join them as soon as he finished his ordination require-ments.) This small group of young men would practice serious spiritual disciplines of prayer, Bible study, accountability and sharing the gospel while on board the ship. They hoped this would prepare them for fruitful work in Georgia when they arrived some five months later. But by January winter storms overtook their ship—and John Wesley got a serious look at his own faith.

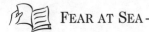 FEAR AT SEA ————————————————————

JOURNAL OF JOHN WESLEY, 1735-1736

Friday, October 31, 1735. We sailed out of the Downs. At eleven at night I was waked by a great noise. I soon found there was no danger. But the bare apprehension of it gave me a lively conviction what manner of men those ought to be who are every moment on the brink of eternity. . . .

Saturday, January 17, 1736. Many people were very impatient at the contrary wind. At seven in the evening they were quieted by a storm. It rose higher and higher till nine. About nine the sea broke over us from stem to stern, burst through the windows of the state cabin where three or four of us were, and covered us all over, though a bureau sheltered me from the main shock. About eleven I lay down in the great cabin, and in a short time fell asleep, though very uncertain whether I should wake alive, and much ashamed of my unwillingness to die. O how pure in heart must he be who would rejoice to appear before God at a moment's warning! Toward morning 'He rebuked the winds and the sea, and there was a great calm.' . . .

Friday, January 23, 1736. In the evening another storm began. In the morning it increased, so that they were forced to let the ship drive. I could not but say to myself, 'How is it that thou has no faith?' being still unwilling to die. About one in the afternoon, almost as soon as I had stepped out of the great cabin door, the sea did not break as usual, but came with a full, smooth tide over the side of the ship. I was vaulted over with water in a moment, and so stunned that I scarce expected to lift up my head again till the sea should give up her dead. But, thanks be to God, I received no hurt at all. About midnight the storm ceased.

Sunday, July 25, 1736. At noon our third storm began. At four it was more violent than any before. Now indeed we could say, 'The waves of the sea were mighty and raged horribly.' They 'rose up to the heavens above, and clave down to hell beneath'. The winds roared round about us, and (what I never heard before) whistled as distinctly as if it had been a human voice, but shook and jarred with so unequal, grating a motion, that one could not but with great difficulty keep one's hold of anything, nor stand a moment without it. Every ten minutes came a shock against the stern or side of the ship, which one would think should dash the planks in pieces. At this time a child, privately baptized before, was brought to be received into the Church. It put me in mind of Jeremiah's buying the field when the Chaldeans were on the point of destroying Jerusalem, and seemed a pledge of the mercy of God designed to show us, even in the land of the living. . . .

At seven I went to the Germans [Moravians]. . . . In the midst of the psalm wherewith their service began the sea broke over, split the mainsail in pieces, covered the ship, and poured in between the decks, as if the great deep had already swallowed us up. A terrible screaming began among the English. The Germans calmly sung on. I asked one of them afterwards, 'Was you not afraid?' He answered, 'I thank God, no.' I asked, 'But were not your women and children afraid?' He replied mildly, 'No; our women and children are not afraid to die.'

From them I went to their crying, trembling neighbours, and pointed out to them the difference in the hour of trial between him that feareth God and him that feareth him not. At twelve the wind fell. This was the most glorious day which I have ever hitherto seen.

 GROUP DISCUSSION OR PERSONAL REFLECTION——

1. January storms at sea brushed Wesley with the smell of death. When have you thought that your own death might be near?

2. What did you gain (or lose) from that experience?

3. By taking another look at his last paragraph above, consider the way John Wesley responded to his scare. Why might fear of God encourage us to also love him?

 INTO THE WORD ————————————————————

4. *Read Matthew 14:22-36.* Put all five of your senses into this scene. What do you see, hear, taste, and so on?

5. Several times this passage speaks of fear. What all was there to be afraid of?

6. What could Peter know about Jesus at the end of this day that he might not have known at the beginning?

7. What are some of your own fears?

8. Verse 31 says that Jesus reached out his hand and caught Peter. In what ways do you see Christ reaching toward you, even during your fears?

9. Why do you think Jesus invited Peter to come to him?

10. How do these events help define the relationship between Jesus and his disciples?

11. What do you see in this story that shows Jesus extending an encouraging kind of love to his disciples?

12. What do you know about Jesus that encourages you?

 ALONG THE ROAD ───────────────────────

Read or sing Charles Wesley's hymn "I Know That My Redeemer Lives" as an act of worship. Select several phrases from the hymn as a basis for continued prayer.

I Know That My Redeemer Lives

I know that my Redeemer lives,
and ever prays for me;
a token of his love he gives,
a pledge of liberty.

I find him lifting up my head:
he brings salvation near;
his presence makes me free indeed
and he will soon appear.

He wills that I should holy be:
who can withstand his will?
The counsel of his grace in me
he surely shall fulfil.

Jesus, I hang upon your Word:
I steadfastly believe
you will return and claim me, Lord,
and to yourself receive.

Charles Wesley, 1742

All of us fear death to some degree (as did John Wesley and the apostle Peter). What encouragement do you find in this hymn that helps you deal with that fear?

◿ Bring to mind several of your major fears. One by one turn these over to your loving Lord, the Son of God, who is able to walk on water and offers you his hand as support.

◿ Who do you know who could use encouragement? Consider what you could do that would be uniquely encouraging to that person in his or her current position. Then share the love of Christ in that way.

II

AMAZING LOVE
Psalm 90

*H*ave you ever made such a mess of your life that you wondered if even God, with all of his power to forgive, could take you in? John Wesley had just returned from St. Simons Island, Georgia, to his home in England. He had hoped to be a light for the gospel in America. Instead he left in disgrace after only two years, having created friction in the church and sadness in a young lady's heart. His journal entries set in England, just prior to the one below, recount one preaching episode after another, each ending with the same refrain: "I am to preach there no more." Yet even while drawing courage to preach under such hostile conditions, Wesley wrestled in his own soul about whether he himself was among the redeemed. Surely he was not good enough to be loved by a holy God. And then he went to Aldersgate.

 A HEART STRANGELY WARMED ──────

JOURNAL OF JOHN WESLEY, 1738

Friday, May 19, 1738. Monday, Tuesday, and Wednesday, I had continual sorrow and heaviness in my heart. . . .

Wednesday, May 24, 1738. I think it was about five this morning, that I opened my Testament . . . "There are given unto us exceeding great and precious promises, even that ye should be partakers of the divine nature. Just as I went out, I opened it again on those words, "Thou art not far from the kingdom of God" [Mk. 12:34]. In the afternoon I was asked to go to St Paul's. The anthem was "Out of the deep have I called unto thee, O Lord: Lord, hear my voice. O let thine ears consider well the voice of my complaint. If thou, Lord, will be extreme to mark what is done amiss, O Lord, who may abide it? For there is mercy with thee; therefore shalt thou be feared. O Israel, trust in the Lord, for with the Lord there is mercy and with him is plenteous redemption. And he shall redeem Israel from all his sins."

In the evening I went very unwillingly to a society in Aldersgate Street, where one was reading Luther's Preface to the Epistle to the Romans. About a quarter before nine, while he was describing the change which God works in the heart through faith in Christ, I felt my heart strangely warmed. I felt I did trust in Christ, Christ alone for salvation; and an assurance was given me that he had taken away *my* sins, even *mine,* and saved *me* from the law of sin and death.

I began to pray with all my might for those who had in a more especial manner despitefully used me and persecuted me. I then testified openly to all there what I now first felt in my heart. But it was not long before the enemy suggested, "This cannot be faith, for where is thy joy?" Then was I taught that "peace and victory over sin are essential to faith in the Captain of our salvation but that, as to the transports of joy—that usually attend the beginning of it especially in those who have mourned deeply—God sometimes giveth, sometimes witholdest them, according to the counsels of his own will."

After my return home, I was much buffeted with temptations, but cried out and they fled away. They returned again and again. I as often lifted up my eyes and he "sent me help from his holy place" [*cf.* Ps. 20:2, B.C.P.]. And herein I found [in what] the difference between this and my former state chiefly consisted. I was striving, yea, fighting with all my might under the law, as well as under grace. But then I was sometimes, if not often, conquered; now, I was always conqueror.

Thursday, May 25, 1738. The moment I awaked, "Jesus, Master," was in my heart and in my mouth; and I found all my strength lay in keeping my eye fixed upon him, and my soul waiting on him continually. Being again at St. Paul's in the afternoon, I could taste the good word of God in the anthem, which began, "My song shall be always of the lovingkindness of the Lord: with my mouth will I ever be showing forth thy truth from one generation to another" [Ps. 89:1, B.C.P.]. Yet the enemy injected a fear, "If thou doest believe, why is there not a more sensible change?" I answered (yet not I): "That I know not. But this I know, I have *now peace with God.* And I *sin not today,* and Jesus my Master has forbid me to take thought for the morrow.". . .

Wednesday, June 7, 1738. I determined, if God should permit, to retire for a short time into Germany. I had fully proposed before I left Georgia so to do, if it should please God to bring me back to Europe. And I now clearly saw the time was come. My weak mind could not bear to be thus sawn asunder. And I hoped the conversing with those holy men who were themselves living witnesses of the full power of faith and yet able to bear with those that are weak, would be a means, under God, of so establishing my soul, that I might "go on from faith to faith and from strength to strength."

(John Wesley spent the next three months in Germany visiting the Moravians.)

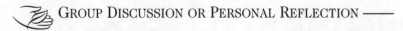 GROUP DISCUSSION OR PERSONAL REFLECTION ——

1. This section from John Wesley's journal records a variety of ways in which he searched for God. What are some of the ways that you have searched for God?

2. Wesley was finally able to believe that God had taken away his sins when his "heart was strangely warmed." When and how has God made his presence known to you?

3. When John Wesley had trouble hanging on to his faith, he went to the Moravians for help. How have other Christians helped maintain your faith?

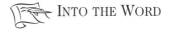 INTO THE WORD ───────────────────

4. *Read Psalm 90.* This psalm begins with the words, "Lord, you have been our dwelling place." Why would you want to *dwell* with God as he is described here?

5. What reasons would you have to also hold God in awe or even fear?

6. Focus on verses 1-6. What images here help you to see that God's presence in time is different from our own?

7. If you were entering a time of discouragement (as John Wesley did), what comfort would you find in these verses?

8. Focus on verses 7-12. John Wesley had a great desire to live a holy life. What do you see in this section of Psalm 90 that would cause you to be concerned about offending God?

9. After describing our brief time on earth (v. 10), this psalm asks that God "teach us to number our days aright" (v. 12). Make a quick calculation of the approximate number of days you have lived. If each day were one dollar, what could you buy?

What could you not buy?

10. Our days are limited (numbered), yet each one is a precious gift from God. We are wise to know its value but also its limitations. How can you use this current day in a way that has lasting value?

11. Focus on verses 13-17. What blessings does Moses ask for?

12. Verse 14 speaks of God's "unfailing love," which can lead us to sing for joy—and in the process get a good start on one of the precious days he has given us. What are some examples you have seen of God's love at work?

 ALONG THE ROAD

John Wesley used his journal to record his memories and hopes and also to testify of God's work in his life. Using verse 14 as a base, write a couple of paragraphs about a past event that mirrors this verse. Or write your hopes for a future time when this verse will become true for you.

Consider the work you have done and are doing. Use verse 17 to help you pray about the impact of your work.

✐ A supreme example of God's love is the work of Jesus Christ on our behalf. Sing or pray your praise for that love using the Charles Wesley hymn "And Can It Be That I Should Gain." Pray a response to God's "amazing love" as it is described in this song.

And Can It Be That I Should Gain

And can it be that I should gain
An int'rest in the Savior's blood?
Died He for me, who caused His pain?
For me, who Him to death pursued?

Amazing love!
how can it be
That Thou, my God shouldst die for me?

He left His Father's throne above,
So free, so infinite His grace!
Emptied Himself of all but love,
And bled for Adam's helpless race!
'Tis mercy all, immense and free,
For, O my God, it found out me.

Long my imprisoned spirit lay
Fast bound in sin and nature's night.
Thine eye diffused a quick'ning ray:
I woke—the dungeon flamed with light!
My chains fell off,
My heart was free,
I rose, went forth, and followed Thee.

No condemnation now I dread:
Jesus, and all in Him, is mine!
Alive in Him, my living Head,
And clothed in righteousness divine,
Bold I approach th' eternal throne,
And claim the crown, thru Christ my own.

Amazing love!
how can it be
That Thou, my God, shouldst die for me!

Charles Wesley, 1738

III

REDEEMING
LOVE

1 John 3:1-10

What happens when God comes into a life and makes it his own? What difference does it make—theologically, emotionally, practically? Are we the same person inside? Do we think and feel the same way? How are we different in our relationship with God? Do we know him in any different way? What about the way we spend our time, make decisions or manage relationships? Are we different than we would have been?

John Wesley was an English Anglican at a time when the established church had grown cold (in his estimation). The wealthy paid fees to rent a pew in their local church, yet they rarely attended. And even if they did attend, many did not take their faith past the church door. Meanwhile, the poor, who could not afford to rent pews, were excluded. So John Wesley took his sermons to the fields and to the mines beginning as early as 5:00 a.m. so as not to conflict with either work schedules or service times of the parish church. Hundreds of workers gathered in the fields to hear him preach of something called "new birth." And this gift from God was available to them! Meanwhile, the wealthy began to squirm uncomfortably in their padded pews. For some, new birth didn't sound like anything they had experienced or perhaps even wanted.

 HOW TO BE TRULY ALIVE

THE NEW BIRTH, 1760

Before a child is born into the world doesn't he have eyes, but does not see? Doesn't he have ears, but does not hear? He has a very imperfect use of the other senses. He has no knowledge of any of the things of the world, nor any natural understanding. . . . But as soon as the child is born, he begins to breathe and live in a wholly different way than before. He begins to see the light and to recognize various objects around him. Hearing is activated, and he hears different sounds striking his ears. All the other organs of sense begin to work in their own spheres.

Listen to the profound analogy at work here! While we are in a mere natural state, before we are born of God, we have, in a spiritual sense, the rudiments of eyes, but see nothing. It is as if a thick, impenetrable veil were pulled over them. We have ears, but we hear nothing; and we are most deaf precisely to that which we most need to hear. Our other spiritual senses are all locked up. We are in the same condition as if we did not even have them. Therefore, we are without knowledge of God, are not in communication with God, are not at all acquainted with God. We have no reliable knowledge of the things of God, of the Spirit and eternity. Though one is a living person, one is not yet alive as a Christian.

As soon as one is born of God, there is a total change in all these ways. . . .

Believers feel, and are inwardly sensible of, the gifts which the Spirit of God is eliciting in their hearts. They feel, and are conscious of, a "peace of God, which is beyond our utmost understanding" (Phil. 4:7) and are "transported with a joy too great for words" (I Pet. 1:8). "Such a hope is no mockery, because God's love has flooded our inmost heart through the Holy Spirit he has given us"

(Rom. 5:5). Thus, they are able to exercise all their spiritual senses to discern spiritual good and evil. By the use of these senses, they daily increase in the knowledge of God, of Jesus Christ whom God has sent, and of everything pertaining to his inward kingdom. . . .

Such a person may be properly said to be alive; God having awakened him by his Spirit, he is alive to God through Jesus Christ, He lives a life the world does not understand, a life that "lies hidden with Christ in God" (Col. 3:3). God is continually breathing life into the soul, and the soul is returning the breath of life to God. Grace is descending into his heart, while his prayer and praise ascend to heaven. By this communion between God and the person, this fellowship with the Father and the Son, as by a kind of spiritual respiration, the life of God in the soul is sustained. In this way the children of God grow up until they attain to a maturity "measured by nothing less than the full stature of Christ" (Eph. 4:13).

At this point we can state plainly the essential nature of the new birth. It is the great change that God works in the soul who brings it into life, when he raises it from the death of sin to the life of righteousness. It is the change made in the whole soul by the almighty Spirit of God when it is "created in Christ Jesus" (Eph. 2:10); when it is "made new in mind and spirit," having "put on the new nature of God's creating, which shows itself in the just and devout life called for by the truth" (Eph. 4:24); when the love of the world is changed into the love of God, pride into humility, passion into meekness, hatred and malice into a sincere, tender, disinterested love for all mankind. In a word, it is that change in which the earthly, sensual, demeaned mind is transformed into the mind which was in Christ Jesus (Phil. 2:5). This is the nature of the new birth. So it is "with everyone who is born from spirit" (John 3:8).

 GROUP DISCUSSION OR PERSONAL REFLECTION ──────

1. Why would you want new birth as it is described here?

2. Why might some people hesitate to come into this relationship with God?

3. Wesley describes a person who has received new birth with the words "such a person may be properly said to be alive." In what ways are you more "alive" because of your relationship with Christ?

 INTO THE WORD ────────────────────

4. *Read 1 John 3:1-10.* What all can you know about new birth from this passage?

5. What, according to this chapter, are the evidences that a person has been born again?

6. Focus on verses 2-3. Notice the hope that is offered here. What is the cause, and what is the effect of that hope?

7. What do you particularly enjoy about this hope?

8. John makes strong statements in this passage about sin in the life of a supposed Christian. How do you deal with these warnings?

9. What are some recommendations you could give Christians that might help us live in a way that pleases God?

10. According to verse 8, Christ's coming was "to destroy the work of the devil." Yet we see evidence that Satan remains alive and well. What do you think John meant?

11. This passage speaks of being "children of God" (vv. 1-2) and "born of God" (v. 9). What do these terms suggest about the relationship between God and those he has redeemed?

12. As you reflect on your own relationship with God, what emotional impact do these phrases have on you?

13. Verse 1 opens with "How great is the love the Father has lavished on us." In what ways is God's redeeming love a "lavish" form of love?

14. Verse 10 says that Christians are to mirror God's love by loving each other. What are some practical ways that you can express that love?

ALONG THE ROAD————————————————————

In view of the 1 John passage, take a sober look at the tolerance you extend to yourself regarding sin. Make any appropriate confessions to God.

Charles Wesley's hymn "O for a Thousand Tongues to Sing" is a hymn of praise for God's redeeming love. Sing or read this hymn.

O for a Thousand Tongues to Sing

O for a thousand tongues to sing
my great Redeemer's praise,
the glories of my God and King,
the triumphs of his grace.

My gracious master and my God,
assist me to proclaim,
to spread through all the earth abroad
the honors of thy name.

Jesus, the name that charms our fears,
that bids our sorrows cease;
'tis music in the sinner's ears,
'tis life and health and peace.

He breaks the pow'r of reigning sin,
he sets the pris'ner free:
his blood can make the foulest clean,
his blood availed for me.

He speaks and, list'ning to his voice,
new life the dead receive;
the mournful, broken hearts rejoice;
the humble poor believe.

Hear him, ye dear; his praise, ye dumb,
your loosen'd tongues employ;
ye blind, behold your Savior come;
and leap, ye lame, for joy.

Charles Wesley, 1739

In what different ways does Charles Wesley illustrate the new life begun at new birth?

Read again verses one and two of the hymn. Ask God to make you aware of opportunities today to use your tongue (or pen or computer keyboard) to proclaim his praise.

IV
ACTIVE LOVE
Philippians 2:1-13

*W*ho is a Christian? That question raised as much ire in John Wesley's circles as it does in our own—particularly if we suspect that the person asking that question might exclude us. It was one of the questions that brought friction between Wesley and the Church of England.

In the "bad old days" of Wesley's England, the underclass endured slave trade, severe poverty, mob riots, festering prisons, ruthless laws (you could be hanged for cutting down a tree) and enforced illiteracy. Yet the church was largely silent on these social ills as well as on qualities of personal integrity. One writer of the era complained that, when compared to people in other occupations, the English clergy were "the most remiss of their labors in private, and the least severe in their lives." It is small wonder that Wesley's intense standards for personal piety did not receive a kind reception within the established church.

Yet Wesley made every effort to follow them himself. A glimpse of Wesley in his middle years would find a small man in old clothes, astride a borrowed horse, reading the writings of Horace in Latin or perhaps scribbling notes for his third sermon of the day in his personally devised shorthand—and it would only have been midmorning. One of his journal entries from 1753 complains that, though his audience at 6:30 a.m. was large, the children made noise and the "grown persons were talking aloud almost all the time I was preaching. It was quite otherwise at five in the morning. There was a large congregation again; and every person therein seemed to know this was the Word whereby God would judge them in the last day."

Wesley wrote "A Plain Account of Genuine Christianity" as a tract, but he probably also used it as a sermon. We can picture him standing on a pile of rocks at 5:00 a.m., in the chilly morning mist, preaching these words in clear, reasoned, almost loving tones to soot-streaked miners headed for work. His opening paragraphs raise questions as to whether they, or anyone they knew, were genuine followers of the Christian faith. But by the end they cannot miss the contentment, joy and hope that Wesley had found in his loving Lord. He offered the same to them—and to us.

 WHO IS A CHRISTIAN? ———————————————

A PLAIN ACCOUNT OF GENUINE CHRISTIANITY, 1753

1. Who is a Christian indeed? What does that term properly imply? It has been so long abused, I fear [it means] nothing at all. . . .

2. A "Christian" cannot think of the Author of his being without abasing himself before him, without a deep sense of the distance between a worm of earth and him that "sitteth on the circle of the heavens," . . . so that he can only cry out, from the fulness of his heart, "O God, what is man? What am I?"

3. He has a continual sense of his dependence on the parent of good, for his being and all the blessings that attend it. To him he refers every natural and every moral endowment, with all that is commonly ascribed either to fortune or to the wisdom, courage, or merit of the possessor. . . . He willingly resigns all he is, all he has, to

his wise and gracious disposal. . . .

4. And as he has the strongest affection for the fountain of all good, so he has the firmest confidence in him; a confidence which neither pleasure nor pain, neither life nor death, can shake. But yet this, far from creating sloth or indolence, pushes him on to the most vigorous industry. . . . And as he knows the most acceptable worship of God is to imitate him he worships, so he is continually labouring to transcribe into himself all his imitable perfections: in particular, his justice, mercy and truth, so eminently displayed in all his creatures.

5. Above all, remembering that God is love, he is conformed to the same likeness. He is full of love to his neighbour: of universal love, not confined to one sect or party, nor restrained to those who agree with him in opinions, or in outward modes of worship, or to those who are allied to him by blood or recommended by nearness of place. Neither does he love those only that love him, or that are endeared to him by intimacy of acquaintance. But his love resembles that of him whose mercy is over all his works. [*cf.* Ps. 145:9, B.C.P.] It . . . [embraces] neighbours and strangers, friends and enemies; yea, not only the good and gentle but also the froward, the evil and unthankful. For he loves every soul that God has made. . . .

6. His love to these, so to all mankind, is in itself generous and disinterested, springing from no view of advantage to himself . . . . By experience he knows that *social love* (if it means the love of our neighbour) is absolutely, essentially different from *self-love,* even of the most allowable kind, just as different as the objects at which they point. . . .

7. And this universal, disinterested love is productive of all right affections. . . . It makes a Christian rejoice in the virtues of all, and bear a part in their happiness at the same time that he sympathizes with their pains and compassionates their infirmities. . . .

8. The same love constrains him to converse, not only with a strict regard to truth but with artless sincerity and genuine simplicity, as one in whom there is no guile . . . in all his conversations

aiming at this, either to improve himself in knowledge or virtue, or to make those with whom he converses some way wiser, or better, or happier than they were before.

9. The same love is productive of all right actions. It . . . makes him invariably resolved in every circumstance of life to do that, and that only, to others, which supposing he were himself in the same situation, he would desire they should do to him.

10. And as he is easy to others, so he is easy in himself. He is free from the painful swellings of pride, from the flames of anger, from the impetuous gusts of irregular self-will. He is no longer tortured with envy or malice, or with unreasonable and hurtful desire. He is no more enslaved to the pleasures of sense, but has the full power both over his mind and body, in a continued cheerful course of sobriety, of temperance and chastity. . . . He stands steady and collected in himself.

11. And he who seeks no praise cannot fear dispraise. Censure gives him no uneasiness, being conscious to himself that he would not willingly offend and that he has the approbation of the Lord of all. He cannot fear want, knowing in whose hand is the earth and the fulness thereof and that it is impossible for him to withhold from one that fears him any manner of thing that is good. He cannot fear pain, knowing it will never be sent unless it is for his real advantage, and that then his strength will be proportioned to it, as it has always been in times past. He cannot fear death, being able to trust him he loves with his soul as well as his body, yea, glad to leave the corruptible body in the dust, 'till it is raised, incorruptible and immortal. So that, in honour or shame, in abundance or want, in ease or pain, in life or in death, always and in all things, he has learned to be content, to be easy, thankful, joyful, happy.

12. He is happy in knowing there is a God—an intelligent Cause and Lord of all—and that he is not the produce either of blind chance or inexorable necessity. . . .

13. He takes knowledge of the invisible things of God, even his eternal power and wisdom in the things that are seen, the heavens,

the earth, the fowls of the air, the lilies of the field. How much more, while rejoicing in the constant care which he still takes of the work of his own hand, he breaks out in a transport of love and praise, "O Lord our Governor! How excellent is thy Name in all the earth; thou that hast set thy glory above the heavens" [Ps. 8:1, B.C.P.]!—while he, as it were, sees the Lord sitting upon his throne and ruling all things well. . . .

14. He is peculiarly and inexpressibly happy in the clearest and fullest conviction: "This all-powerful, all-wise, all-gracious Being, this Governor of all, loves *me*. This lover of my soul is always with me, is never absent; no, not for a moment. And I love him: there is none in heaven but thee, none on earth that I desire beside thee [*cf.* Ps. 73:25]! And he has given me to resemble himself; he has stamped his image on my heart. And I live unto him; I do only his will; I glorify him with my body and my spirit. And it will not be long before I shall die unto him, I shall die into the arms of God. And then farewell sin and pain, then it only remains that I should live with him for ever."

15. This is the plain, naked portraiture of a Christian. But be not prejudiced against him for his name. Forgive his particularities of opinion and (what you think) superstitious modes of worship. These are circumstances but of small concern and do not enter into the essence of his character. Cover them with a veil of love and look at the substance: his tempers, his holiness, his happiness. Can calm reason conceive either a more amiable or a more desirable character?

Is it your own? Away with names! Away with opinions! I care not what you are called. I ask not (it does not deserve a thought) what opinion you are of, so you are conscious to yourself that you are the man whom I have been (however faintly) describing.

Do not you know you ought to be such? Is the Governor of the world well pleased that you are not?

Do you at least desire it? I would to God that desire may penetrate your inmost soul and that you are not only almost but altogether a Christian.

GROUP DISCUSSION OR PERSONAL REFLECTION ——

1. What is your initial reaction to Wesley's description of a genuine Christian?

2. Give a title to each of Wesley's fifteen paragraphs—or circle a key phrase that summarizes or highlights its content. What do you find to respect about Wesley's description of a genuine Christian?

3. What personal challenges do you find in Wesley's essay?

 INTO THE WORD ——————————————————

4. *Read Philippians 2:1-13.* What similarities do you see between this section of Paul's letter to the church at Philippi and Wesley's description of a genuine Christian?

5. Verses 1-4 speak of two kinds of unity. What are some ways that our unity with Christ is likely to show itself in our character (v. 1)?

6. In what practical ways can we show the unity we have with other Christians (vv. 2-4)?

7. When and how have you seen these unifying characteristics in action?

8. Thoughtfully reread verses 3-8. Bring to mind one of your most important relationships. In what specific ways could you follow the pattern established by Jesus?

9. Focus on verses 9-11. How do you want to respond to Jesus as he is described here?

10. Paul says in verse 12 that we are to "work out our salvation with fear and trembling." Using this excerpt from Paul's letter as well as the Wesley essay, how could you go about this task?

11. In paragraphs 2 and 3 of "Plain Account," Wesley describes a Christian as one who has an accurate view of self along with an accurate view of God. How does Philippians 2 help you with that understanding?

12. Read aloud paragraph 14 of Wesley's essay. Wesley says that at the end of his journey, "I shall die into the arms of God." How does this hope influence some of your own thoughts about life—and death?

 ALONG THE ROAD────────────────────────

John Wesley outlined "methods" of living the Christian faith. At one point his method was to examine himself for sin once every hour! Create a method of your own—perhaps less strenuous than Wesley's personal pattern. Select one paragraph from his essay above and try to live it for one day. At the end of the day examine yourself in prayer. Admit to God your failures. (Be specific.) Rejoice also over your successes and the growth that these represent. If you feel brave, select another paragraph and follow the same pattern for the next day.

2 To what extent does Wesley's picture of a genuine Christian describe you? Wesley asks at the end, "Do you at least desire it?" Write a letter, as if you were writing to John Wesley himself, expressing your response.

2 Sing "Love Divine" as an offering of prayer to God. After singing verse four, ask God to show you specific areas where he wants to finish the work of salvation he has begun in you. In silence submit (as much as you are able) those areas to him. Then sing this stanza again as an offering of yourself.

Love Divine, All Loves Excelling

Love divine, all loves excelling,
Joy of heav'n, to earth come down;
Fix in us Thy humble dwelling,
All Thy faithful mercies crown.
Jesus, Thou are all compassion,
Pure, unbounded love Thou art;
Visit us with Thy salvation,
Enter ev'ry trembling heart.

Breathe, O breathe Thy loving Spirit
Into ev'ry troubled breast!
Let us all in Thee inherit,
Let us find that promised rest.
Take away our bent to sinning,
Alpha and Omega be;
End of faith, as its beginning,
Set our hearts at liberty.

Come, almighty to deliver,
Let us all Thy life receive;
Suddenly return, and never,
Nevermore Thy temples leave.
Thee we would be always blessing,
Serve Thee as Thy hosts above,
Pray and praise Thee without ceasing,
Glory in Thy perfect love.

Finish then Thy new creation,
Pure and spotless let us be;
Let us see Thy great salvation
Perfectly restored in Thee:
Changed from glory into glory,
Till in heav'n we take our place,
Till we cast our crowns before Thee,
Lost in wonder, love and praise! Amen.

Charles Wesley, 1746

V

JOYFUL LOVE
1 Thessalonians 5:12-28

Susanna Wesley gave birth to nineteen children! (She herself was the youngest of twenty-five.) Of her nineteen children, ten died in infancy, including two sets of twins. Even though she grew up in comparative ease and was given a good education by her father, after her marriage to Samuel Wesley she lived most of her life in poverty in a swampy rural town where most adults could not read. Her husband, the town pastor, was so actively disliked that parishioners stabbed their family's cows so that the animals could not give milk, and they may have set fire to their home—which burned down twice. At the second burning the family lost all of their belongings, including Susanna's journals and the lifelong scholarly works of her father. Worse, she had to separate her children to live with various relatives during the year that they were without a home.

Even after the family reunited, Susanna's life was never easy. Her poverty was so severe that the children were limited to one helping of one item of food at each meal; one daughter who was offered a job had to refuse because there was no money to buy a suitable dress. Daughter Mary was crippled; Kessy was possibly retarded; Hetty became pregnant without the benefit of marriage (the child died, as did all of her subsequent children); Samuel, her beloved oldest son, died ahead of her; several children formed disastrous marriages—including John, whose wife was once seen dragging him across the floor by his hair. When Susanna's husband died, her sons had to sell every item belonging to her in order to pay his debts. During the last decade of her life she could rarely leave home due to illness. Yet Susanna Wesley is revered (and rightly so) as a model of wise mothering and godly womanhood. Why? John and Charles Wesley.

In fairness to the other children, several of them (particularly Hetty) might also have led historically significant lives if given the opportunity. But these two sons (numbers sixteen and eighteen in birth sequence) had the benefit of a classical education, begun first at home by their parents and later at Oxford, partially supported by their older brother. Charles inherited (and greatly magnified) his father's gift with poetry. John was more logical and sober (as was his mother) and turned his mind toward theology. Their impoverished surroundings gave them easy communication with rural workers who would later become their parishioners. But a deep faith that would infect their world grew first in their mother's kitchen.

One example comes from an exchange of letters between Susanna and her husband. Reverend Wesley had gone to London for a months-long Convocation of the Established Church. The parish church at Epworth began to flounder in his absence, so Susanna held Sunday evening meetings in her kitchen and notified her husband that she was doing so. A fiery exchange of letters resulted giving a brief sample of Susanna's spiritual strength. Her husband knew when he was bested; Susanna continued her meetings.

These kitchen meetings later became a model for John Wesley's "classes" or accountability groups by which he nourished converts in his revivals. For this and many other reasons Susanna Wesley is titled "The Mother of Methodism."

WORDS FROM SUSANNA ————————————————

SUSANNA WESLEY: THE COMPLETE WRITINGS, 1711-1712

To Samuel Wesley Sr.
6 February 1711/12
. . . I am a woman, so I am also mistress of a large family. And
though the superior charge of the souls contained in it lies upon
you as head of the family and as their minister, yet in your absence
I cannot but look upon every soul you leave under my care as a tal-
ent committed to me under a trust by the great Lord of all the families of heaven and earth. And if I am unfaithful to him or to you in
neglecting to improve these talents, how shall I answer unto him,
when he shall command me to render an account of my steward-
ship? . . .

I resolved to begin with my own children, and accordingly I proposed and observed the following method: I take such a proportion
of time as I can best spare every night to discourse with each child
by itself on something that relates to its principal concerns. On
Monday I talk with Molly, on Tuesday with Hetty, Wednesday with
Nancy, Thursday with Jacky, Friday with Patty, Saturday with
Charles, and with Emily and Sukey together on Sunday.

With those few neighbours who then came to me I discoursed
more freely and affectionately than before. I chose the best and
most awakening sermons we had, and I spent more time with them
in such exercises. Since this our company has increased every
night, for I dare deny none that asks admittance. Last Sunday I
believe we had above two hundred, and yet many went away for
want of room. . . .

To Samuel Wesley Sr.
25 February 1711/12
. . . If you do after all think fit to dissolve this assembly, do not tell
me any more that you desire me to do it, for that will not satisfy my
conscience; but send me your positive command in such full and
express terms as may absolve me from all guilt and punishment for

neglecting this opportunity of doing good to souls, when you and I shall appear before the great and awful tribunal of our Lord Jesus Christ.

I dare not wish this practice of ours had never been begun, but it will be with extreme [?] grief that I shall dismiss them, because I foresee the consequences. I pray God direct and bless you. . . .

Morning [Journal, no date]

Though "man is born to trouble," yet I believe there is scarce a man to be found upon earth, but, take the whole course of his life, hath more mercies than afflictions, and much more pleasure than pain. I am sure it has been so in my case. I have many years suffered much pain and great bodily infirmities; but I have likewise enjoyed great intervals of rest and ease. And those very sufferings have, by the blessing of God, been of excellent use and proved the most proper means of reclaiming me from a vain and sinful conversation, insomuch that I cannot say, I had better have been without this affliction, this disease, this loss, want, contempt, or reproach. All my sufferings, by the admirable management of omnipotent Goodness, have concurred to promote my spiritual and eternal good. And if I have not reaped that advantage by them which I might have done, it is merely owing to the perverseness of my own will and frequent lapses into present things and unfaithfulness to the good Spirit of God, who, notwithstanding all my prevarications, all the stupid opposition I have made, has never totally abandoned me. [Eternal] glory be to thee, O Lord!

Evening [Prayer]

If to esteem and have the highest reverence for thee! if constantly and sincerely to acknowledge thee the supreme, the only desirable Good be to love thee—I do love thee!

If comparatively to despise and undervalue all the world contains, which is esteemed great, fair, or good, if earnestly and constantly to desire thee, thy favour, thy acceptance, thyself rather than all or all things thou has created be to love thee—I do love thee!

If to rejoice in thy essential majesty and glory! If to feel a vital joy overspread and cheer the heart at each perception of thy blessedness, at every thought that thou art God and that all things are in thy power, that there is none superior or equal to thee be to love thee—I do love thee!

 GROUP DISCUSSION OR PERSONAL REFLECTION ——

1. What do you appreciate about Susanna's letters to her husband?

2. Look again at the excerpt from Susanna's journal. What reasons did Susanna have to believe that "man is born to trouble"?

3. How might her attitude about trouble lead her toward joy?

4. Study her evening prayer poem. Mentally picture a typical day for Susanna Wesley. In view of this prayer, how would she express her love for God during that day?

INTO THE WORD

5. *Read 1 Thessalonians 5:16-29.* What do you see here that reminds you of Susanna?

6. Paul uses strong language at the end of this letter to the church at Thessalonica. What words and phrases here seem particularly forceful?

7. What do you think Paul intended his readers to understand from the tone of his final instructions?

8. What do you see here that would be helpful to you? Difficult?

9. Paul begins his instructions with "Be joyful always" (v. 16). If you were to give yourself a letter grade on your current practice of this command, what would you give? Explain. (If in doubt, what grade do you think your family or friends would give you?)

10. How might the rest of the instructions in verses 16-22 lead you toward joy?

11. What does Paul want us to be when Jesus returns (vv. 23-24)?

12. What hope does he (and we) have that this kind of change can happen?

13. How might Paul's closing of verses 25-28 point toward joyful love within the church?

14. What is one step you could take toward a more joyful expression of love to God?

ALONG THE ROAD————————————————————

Susanna Wesley wrote a prayer poem expressing her love of God. Create a repeated line, as she did with "I do love thee," and write your own prayer poem expressing honestly your own worship of God.

Susanna Wesley and her son John each kept extensive journals in which they recorded not only the events of a day but also their spiritual goals, their attempts to meet those goals, their doubts and worries about their relationship with God, as well as records of jubilant praise. Select the topic of joyful love for God. Journal your concerns, attempts, experiences or hopes to love God with joy.

❷ Use Charles Wesley's song "Arise, My Soul, Arise" along with its joyful tune to stir yourself to joyful praise. Let its words remind you of all that it means to be a child of God.

Arise, My Soul, Arise

Arise, my soul, arise,
shake off your guilty fears;
the bleeding Sacrifice
in my behalf appears:
before the throne my Surety stands,
before the throne my Surety stands,
my name is written on his hands.

He ever lives above,
for me to intercede,
his all-redeeming love,
his precious blood to plead;
his blood atoned for ev'ry race,
his blood atoned for ev'ry race,
and sprinkles now the throne of grace.

Five bleeding wounds he bears,
received on Calvary;
they pour effectual prayers,
they strongly plead for me.
"Forgive him, O forgive," they cry,
"forgive him, O forgive," they cry,
"nor let that ransomed sinner die!"

My God is reconciled;
his pard'ning voice I hear;
he owns me for his child,
I can no longer fear;
with confidence I now draw nigh,
with confidence I now draw nigh,
and "Father, Abba, Father!" cry.

Charles Wesley, 1742

VI

ETERNAL LOVE
Romans 8:18-39

John Wesley first met Peggy Dale in March of 1765. Peggy and her two sisters, Molly and Ann, were living with Wesley's friend Miss Lewen. Like many families of the era, the Dales had suffered the death of their father while they were still young; Miss Lewen took them in. Peggy, who was twenty when she met John Wesley, became a regular correspondent with him, with some thirty letters from Wesley addressed to her. At the beginning of their correspondence Wesley was sixty-two years old, and his letters reflect the wisdom of a man who has lived long in God's shadow and invites his young "sister" to do the same.

Yet Peggy Dale thought that her life would be short. Since her father died when she was still a child, we can wonder if some contagious disease (perhaps tuberculosis) infected the family. According to the village records of Newcastle, Peggy lived longer than she had thought possible. She was married to Edward Avison, an organist, in 1773 in a notation that speaks of her as a "spinster" (at age twenty-eight!). But her marriage was short.

Her husband died in October 1776 at age twenty-nine. Peggy Dale Avison died a year later at age thirty-three.

Tombstones of that era were likely to summarize your life; if you were a scoundrel, it was recorded for posterity on your tombstone. But Peggy and Edward's tombstone reads as follows: "In memory of Edward Avison and Margaret his wife, who were eminent for piety and primitive simplicity of manners. Having each borne a lingering disease with the most exemplary patience and resignation, they rejoiced in the approach of death, and expired with hopes full of immortality." We can believe that Peggy Dale's confidence in God's eternal love was nurtured in part by the letters she received from John Wesley.

 LETTERS TO PEGGY DALE ────────────────────

THE LETTERS OF THE REV. JOHN WESLEY, 1765

CASTLEBAR, *June I, 1765.*

MY DEAR MISS PEGGY,—Certainly you not only need not sin, but you need not doubt any more. Christ is yours. All is yours. You can give Him all your heart; and will He not freely give you all things? But you can only return what He has given by continually receiving more. You have reason to bless Him who has cast your lot in a fair ground. Even in this world He does not withhold from you any manner of thing that is good. Let your heart be always open to receive His whole blessing!

How far do you find power over your thoughts? Does not your imagination sometimes wander? Do those imaginations continue for any time? or have you power to check them immediately? Do you find continually the spirit of prayer? and are you always happy? I trust you will be happier every day; and that you will not forget, my dear sister,

Your affectionate brother.

Miss Dale, At the Orphan House,
In Newcastle-upon-Tyne.
By Portpatrick. Pd. Two pence.

LONDON, *November* 6, 1765.

MY DEAR SISTER,—By our intercourse with a beloved friend it often pleases God to enlighten our understanding. But this is only the second point: to warm the heart is a greater blessing than light itself. And this effect I frequently find from your letters. The Lord repay it sevenfold into your own bosom! Do you still remain in the persuasion that you shall not live beyond three-and-twenty? Do you remember when or how it began? Does it continue the same, whether your health is worse or better? What a mercy is it that death has lost its sting! Will this hinder any real or substantial happiness? Will it prevent our loving one another?

> Can Death's interposing tide
> Spirits on in Christ divide?

Surely no! Whatever comes from Him is eternal as Himself.
—My dear sister, adieu!

To Miss Dale, At the Orphan House,
Newcastle-upon Tyne.

LONDON, *December* 31, 1765.

MY DEAR PEGGY,—Whether that persuasion was from nature or from God a little time will show. It will be matter of great joy to me if God gives you many years to glorify Him in the body before He removes you to the world of spirits. The comfort is, that life or death, all is yours, seeing you are Christ's: all is good, all is blessing! You have only to rest upon Him with the whole weight of your soul. Temptations to pride you may have, or to anything; but these do not sully your soul. Amidst a thousand temptations you may retain unspotted purity. Abide in Him by simple faith this moment! Live, walk in love! The Lord increase it in you a thousandfold! Take out of His fullness grace upon grace. Tell me from time [to time] just what you feel. I cannot tell you how tenderly I am, my dear sister, Your affectionate brother.

 GROUP DISCUSSION OR PERSONAL REFLECTION ——

1. Sometimes it's fun to picture the other side of a one-sided conversation. In view of these three letters *to* her, what can you know of Peggy Dale?

2. What encouragement was she likely to find in these letters?

3. The aging Wesley gave brotherly advice to his young friend. What advice here might also be helpful to you?

 INTO THE WORD ——————————————————

4. *Read Romans 8:18-39.* What encouragement would Peggy Dale find in these verses?

5. Wesley's letters draw Peggy Dale's attention to a context far larger than the one in which she lived. What do you see in this passage from Romans that helps you see a bigger perspective than your current scene?

6. Focus on verses 18-25. What connections can you see between God's natural creation and God's human creation?

7. Verses 24 and 25 speak of hope. What hope does this passage offer—hope for ourselves and for our environment?

8. What if you don't feel like praying, don't know how to pray or don't think that you pray well—how might verses 26-27 keep you praying in spite of these problems?

9. Focus on verses 28-30. What are the steps of Christian development?

10. Study the five questions and their explanations in verses 31-38. What threats to normal Christian growth does each question suggest?

11. How does God overcome each of these potential hazards?

12. Three times in these closing verses Paul mentions God's love (vv. 35, 37, 38). If you were feeling weak or powerless, what courage could you draw from this kind of love?

13. Peggy Dale seemed to think that she was about to die—so John Wesley wrote to her of hope even in suffering. How does this passage from Romans bring you hope in your current suffering?

 ALONG THE ROAD————————————————————

Read aloud Romans 8.38-39, stopping after each phrase to acknowledge your fears, worries or doubts in each area. Pray about these. Pray also your thanksgiving. Read the verses aloud again as your personal declaration of faith.

◖ Read aloud "Jesus, Lover of My Soul."

Jesus, Lover of My Soul

Jesus, lover of my soul,
let me to thy bosom fly,
while the nearer waters roll,
while the tempest still is high:
hide me, O my Savior, hide,
till the storm of life is past;
safe into the haven guide,
O receive my soul at last!

Other refuge have I none,
hangs my helpless soul on thee;
leave, ah! Leave me not alone,
still support and comfort me!
All my trust on thee is stayed,
all my help from thee I bring;
cover my defenseless head
with the shadow of thy wing.

Thou, O Christ, art all I want;
more than all in thee I find:
raise the fallen, cheer the faint,
heal the sick, and lead the blind.
Just and holy is thy name;
I am all unrighteousness;
false and full of sin I am,
thou art full of truth and grace.

Plenteous grace with thee is found,
grace to cover all my sin;
let the healing streams abound;
make and keep me pure within:
thou of life the fountain art,
freely let me take of thee;
spring thou up within my heart,
rise to all eternity.

Charles Wesley, 1740

✐ What do you find here that speaks truth about yourself?

✐ Focus on verses 3 and 4 of the hymn. What does it reveal about the eternal nature of Christ's work? Thank God for the work of Jesus on your behalf—as expressed in this hymn.

✐ How does this hymn express some of your own longings? Sing the hymn softly as your prayer.

How to Lead a Christian Classics Bible Study

If you are leading a small group discussion using this series, we have good news for you: you do not need to be an expert on Christian history. We have provided the information you need about the historical background in the introduction to each study. Reading more of the original work of these writers will be helpful but is not necessary. We have set each reading in context within the introductions to each study. Further background and helps are found in the study notes to each session as well. And a bibliography is provided at the end of each guide.

In leading the Bible study portion of each study you will be helped by a resource like *Leading Bible Discussions* in our LifeGuide® Bible Study series as well as books dealing with small group dynamics like *The Big Book on Small Groups*. But, once again, you do not need to be an expert on the Bible. The Bible studies are designed to follow the flow of the passage from observation to interpretation to application. You may feel that the studies lead themselves! The study notes at the back will help you through the tough spots.

What Is Your Job as a Leader?

☐ To pray that God will be at work in your heart and mind as well as in the hearts and minds of the group members.

☐ To thoroughly read all of the studies, Scripture texts and all of the helps in this guide before the study.

☐ To help people to feel comfortable as they arrive and to encourage everyone to participate in the discussion.

☐ To encourage group members to apply what they are learning in the study session and by using the "Along the Road" sections between sessions.

Study Notes

Study One. Encouraging Love. Matthew 14:22-36.
Purpose: To find encouragement from Christ's love that will help us face our fears.
Background. At the age of twenty-two John Wesley discovered Bishop Jeremy Taylor's two-hundred-year-old book *Rules for Holy Living and Dying.* In this Anglican bishop, Wesley found a kindred spirit who listed dozens of practical ways to grow in the personal holiness that he so much desired for his own life. Among these challenges Bishop Taylor admonished true Christians not to waste the time that God had given them. As a check on how we use this gift of time, he suggested that we make notes of how we use each hour of every day. Wesley took the challenge to heart and began a journal. He continued the events of his day (along with commensurate soul searching) all of his life. He did not plague his readers with an hour by hour account of his remaining sixty-six years, but he excerpted portions that he deemed appropriate for the public eye. What began as a personal discipline in making a written account of time ended with a gift, a peek into the soul of a man who knew God and committed himself to constant daily response to God in thought, word and deed.
Question 1. Perhaps you have never been close to death. Then con-

sider this alternative question: If you had been in Wesley's situation, what thoughts would have come into your head?

Question 3. The transition from fear to love may seem extreme, yet Wesley saw it in the Moravians. Because they feared God, they also trusted him for their care, or for their death, whichever he desired. Their fear of God led them to sing songs of praise to him even in the face of mortal uncertainty. Their fear of God (and therefore their trust and love) outweighed their fear of the storm. In future journal entries Wesley spent much time reflecting on his own reaction to the storm as compared to the Moravians. It caused him to reassess his faith and eventually to enter a deeper phase of commitment to Christ.

Question 5. Terms speaking of fear appear several times in verses 26-27, but reasons for fear (and awe) appear throughout the story. Why, for example, did the disciples reach the conclusion voiced in verse 32?

Question 6. Survey the events of this day from the beginning of the chapter in order to answer this question. In view of Jesus' many stresses (beginning with the murder of his cousin) it is small wonder that he needed time alone to pray.

Question 8. Consider also the flip side of this question. Jesus reached his hand toward Peter, but Peter—near to drowning—grabbed on. How can you reach toward Christ in a time of fear?

Question 9. Jesus could have responded to Peter's outrageous request with "Don't be silly; stay in the boat! I'm coming there anyway." But he didn't. Why did he comply with Peter's request? What did Peter gain from that experience?

Study Two. Amazing Love. Psalm 90.

Purpose: To acknowledge God's "unfailing love" and respond in praise and worship as we use the time he has given us for his glory.

Background. John Wesley was thirty-five years old. He had finished a rigorous education, founded The Holy Club at Oxford, been ordained as a pastor in the Church of England, started the Methodist Society and ordained preachers to that society. (The Church of

England wanted no part of Methodist-style evangelism.) He practiced intense spiritual disciplines of prayer, poverty, self-examina-
tion and acts of service—especially to prisoners. He had served two
years as a missionary on St. Simons Island off the coast of Georgia—unsuccessfully, he believed. In spite of all of this work for God,
Wesley agonized about whether his own soul was among the
redeemed.

On the ship headed for Georgia, he had encountered a group of
Moravians. Their beautiful singing and calm faith in God, even
while a storm lashed the boat, caused Wesley to long for their quiet
acceptance and personal trust in God's love. He returned to
England and threw himself into preaching—often three or four
times a day. But his journal shows a tortured search for God's presence in his own life.

Was John Wesley converted at Aldersgate? Or was this experience simply a long-prayed-for assurance of salvation already given
by God some fourteen years earlier while he was a student at
Oxford? Wesley himself, though writing exuberantly about his
Aldersgate experience in his journal at the time, later rarely men-
tioned it. In fact, other later experiences of confidence in God
receive similar attention to this one. During the months surround-
ing Aldersgate, Wesley drew much spiritual strength from the Moravians. But though he spoke respectfully of them, within a year he
came to differ with them on just how important it is to have full
confidence of faith in God. Some Moravians believed that they
should do nothing at all toward God unless they were able to
believe fully in him. Wesley's faith was much more action based.
According to Wesley's later teachings, we believe and act on that
faith, and even if our faith begins to lag, we continue to seek God
and act on his teachings.

Question 1. Notice the variety of places where John Wesley
searched for God as recorded in this section of his journal. Then
review some of your own searches. (Most of us look in far less likely
places than did Wesley.)

Question 4. "Dwelling place" suggests a comfortable spot, a place where it is all right to go to sleep, a place of safety. This psalm describes several aspects of God that would invite us to dwell in him. But it also speaks of his anger and much that is a mystery about God. Use questions 4 and 5 to survey the whole psalm.

Question 7. It is precisely God's timelessness that helps us deal with our own preoccupation with the here and now. Wesley valued time so much that he kept daily records of how he used his time. Yet God is "from everlasting to everlasting" (v. 2). This helps us to see the importance of our life (and the days in it) but also its smallness in God's grand scheme. Knowing that God sees the big picture, even created it, can comfort and encourage us during the hard times when our own time seems far too limited. Bring to mind specific situations in your own experience where the concepts from this section of the psalm might bring comfort.

Question 11. Consider the several blessings that Moses feels free to ask and expect from God in this closing stanza. Regarding the final verse it is interesting to note that a psalm speaking so eloquently of the limitation of our days on earth ends with a prayer that God will "establish" the work of our hands. This is a contrast to Ecclesiastes, where we read similar phrases about the frustration of a short life that is meaningless in the end. Here instead we see that God can and does establish what we do even under the limitations of time assigned to us.

Study Three. Redeeming Love. 1 John 3:1-10.
Purpose: To appreciate the love that God offers through the gift of new birth, and to live by its accompanying hope.
Background. What is the process by which God grants new birth to people? Most of us don't think much about those kinds of questions but theologians do. And John Wesley was not only a preacher, he was also a theologian. John Wesley believed in "prevenient grace." It was not a new concept; he borrowed it from Jacobus Arminius (1560-1609), who in turn had borrowed it from Pelagius (fifth century A.D.) as well as early Christians in Greece. Wesley believed that God offered saving grace to everyone; God even

offered the ability to begin to accept that grace. But God also gave each person the freedom to turn away if he or she desired.

In addition to this view of grace, Wesley also developed a particular view of faith. He believed that saving faith was a gift from God and that this faith was all that was necessary for salvation. But Wesley was careful to define genuine faith. He believed that saving faith would always have two specific results: Saving faith would produce assurance of salvation in the heart of the believer; a true Christian would *know* that he or she belonged to God, that Jesus died for *my* sins. Second, saving faith would produce a holy life; a true believer would live a highly moral life, full of good works, motivated by love for God and love for other people.

These may seem like small distinctions from various other Christian beliefs, but it shaped an uncommon view in Wesley's setting, which was heavily populated by Calvinist influence. The passage from 1 John 3 says much to support Wesley's concept of what saving faith and a redeemed life look like.

Question 3. Consider several aspects of aliveness. Think of experiences when you felt particularly alive. Consider also what it means to be alive in your relationship with other Christians, particularly as you step into their lives and share their joy as well as their sadness. Then consider what it means to be alive in an eternal sense.

Question 4. Survey the entire passage to gain a general sense of new birth. Save more specific information for the next question.

Question 5. Find information in almost every verse, particularly verses 1, 2, 3, 6, 7, 9, 10.

Question 6. The cause of hope takes up most of verses 2 and 3. The effect comes at the end of verse 3, but then sets up the topic for the next seven verses.

Question 10. John does not give us a specific answer to this question. It may help to reflect on Satan's role in our temptations to sin. Consider also the influence of Christ's death and resurrection on Satan's goals. Add to this your understanding of what Scripture teaches about Satan's final outcome.

Study Four. Active Love. Philippians 2:1-13.
Purpose: To become more and more Christian by imitating Christ.
Background. John Wesley's essay, "A Plain Account," began as a theological dispute. In 1749 Dr. Conyers Middleton, a deist teaching at Cambridge, published an essay to the effect that Protestants ought to pay attention to the Scripture and not to the lives and teachings of ancient Christians. In fact, Middleton attempted to prove that nothing miraculous had happened since the New Testament age and (by implication) perhaps not even then. The result of the paper was to cast doubt on the character of all Christians prior to the Reformation.

Wesley saw this as a threat to the connection of the current church with Christians of the past and to the supernatural work of God in bringing salvation. So he set about composing an answer. He wrote, "I postponed my voyage and spent almost twenty days in the unpleasing employment." The result was a sixty-page explanation of the works and writings of Christians between the age of the New Testament era and the Reformation. Critics were not impressed. Wesley's work was done too quickly and without the careful scholarship needed to refute Middleton's essay. His sixty pages were soon forgotten.

But there is a footnote to this story. Wesley was convinced that the validity of the Christian faith was not in ancient stories and proofs of miracles (or their lack) but in the lives of God's people. This life of faith, in people of the present, past and future spoke more strongly for the power of God than any miracles. Their lives formed a connecting link between the pages of Scripture and the illustrated grace of God. So at the end of his sixty pages of academic argument, Wesley wrote a short essay about what it means to be a real Christian. "A Plain Account of Genuine Christianity" is thought by some to be the most compelling writing of his life.

Question 8. As you consider your part in this relationship, consider Christ's actions (and your own) using these phrases from the text: "did not consider equality" (v. 6), "made himself nothing" (v. 7), "nature of a servant" (v. 7), "humbled himself" (v. 8), "death" (v. 8).

Question 9. Several phrases from the text may help you grasp this scene: "name" (v. 9), "bow" (v. 10), "in heaven and on earth and under the earth" (v. 10), "every tongue" (v. 11), "Jesus Christ is Lord" (v. 11), "glory" (v. 11). Take a few moments to reflect on these phrases before framing your response.

Question 10. Must we work in order to earn our salvation? Must we live the life of "genuine Christianity" in order to pay our way into God's family. "No," says Francis Foulkes, writing in *New Bible Commentary* (ed. I. Howard Marshall et. al [Downers Grove, Ill.: Inter-Varsity Press, 1994], p. 1254). "*Work out* here has the sense of bringing to completion. It is not a matter of working *for* salvation. We could never do that. The very word *salvation* (which means 'rescue') signifies that we cannot save ourselves (*cf.* Jn. 15:4-5; 1 Cor. 15:10; Eph. 2:5, 8), but we can and must live lives that show God's saving power that we have made our own. We have our part to do, but that is made possible by God's work in us. . . . He gives both the desire and the strength to do what is pleasing to him."

Study Five. Joyful Love. 1 Thessalonians 5:12-28.
Purpose: To praise God with joyful love.
Background. Susanna's era was a challenging time for English women. On the one hand, marvels in art and science threaded through the nation. Halley was doing astronomy; Christopher Wren was building great architecture; Handel, composer of *The Messiah,* now lived in England. But the Anglican Church was in decline. Decades of fighting about which fragment should be the official church, along with general moral corruption, turned the church into a social convenience rather than God at work in the midst of his people. In fact, the great thrust of science had also influenced theology. Deism was a favorite belief, with its idea that God had created the universe but had now retired to some distant spot to let people govern their own lives. Cold logic, deists believed, was the most important way to come to truth. God was not a god of the heart.

All of this had little direct influence on women—particularly in rural areas. These women did not go to school—as did few men, for that matter. One of the reasons that Susanna read her husband's sermons at her kitchen meetings during his absence was that no man in the parish could read without having to spell out most of the words. A few women, including Susanna and her daughters, learned at home. Hetty, for example, was reading the Greek New Testament at the age of eight. Susanna's father, a capable scholar, had taught her much that a son would learn. But sons, if their family could afford it, went to school by the time they were fourteen. Daughters by that time had better be thinking about marriage, for it was primarily through marriage that a woman could find a place in life. If unmarried, the best she could hope would be dependence on other family members or perhaps service as a governess (if educated) or a maid.

Medical care also was limited. A pregnancy each year was common. Midwives, often elderly women without other financial support (or training), assisted at births. Many women died in childbirth, as did Susanna's daughter Mary, one of the few of her six daughters who had a happy marriage. In fact, the church offered a special service for women who survived giving birth. It was called "churching" or "The Thanksgiving of Women After Childbirth." Sad to say, many had little to feel thankful about since some 50 percent of their babies would die, as did ten of Susanna's—one accidentally smothered by a nurse several weeks after surviving birth. At one point Susanna suffered the birth and death of a baby five years in a row. (The next year John was born.) Though Susanna endured much sadness (and wrote about it), she was also able to focus on joy. She was a woman of strong faith—and that faith made her strong.

Question 6. Notice superlatives throughout this passage: "always" (v. 16), "continually" (v. 17), "all" (v. 18), "everything" (v. 21), "every" (v. 22), "through and through" (v. 23), "whole" (v. 23). These words, along with the tense short tone, create a cumulative effect of urgency.

Question 12. The surface answer to this question is obvious from verse 24. But thoughtfully consider what each of the three phrases of that verse means. How do these qualities of God bring you hope about the preceding verse?

Question 13. The "holy kiss" of verse 25 brings smiles today. A kiss (perhaps on both cheeks) was a familiar greeting in that culture, similar to our handshake or hug. It did not imply sexual overtones.

Question 14. Paul's instructions throughout verses 16-28 may trigger some ideas of where to begin cultivating joy. Look again at each one to see if it brings to mind a specific action, habit or thought pattern that could lead you toward a more joyful expression of love for God.

Study Six. Eternal Love. Romans 8:18-39.

Purpose: To find courage and hope in God's eternal love.

Background. John Wesley wrote hundreds of letters in his lifetime. Some of them were mini-sermons. Some were theological treatises. Some were defenses of his work as a revivalist. But many were nurturing letters of discipleship. In this series of letters to the young, sickly Peggy Dale, Wesley leads her to accept her life with all of its uncertainties, anchor her faith in God and anticipate with joy the life to come.

Question 5. We all get bogged down in what we can see, our own here-and-now. Yet if we are to have any hope at all, we must get beyond that. "Hope that is seen is no hope at all" (v. 24). This section of Romans is full of perspective shifts. Notice events that are past, blended with the present, and mixed with the future. Examples include nature that "groans," suffering (unheard) alongside us (vv. 19-22). We ourselves have a context bigger than we can see. We are already children of God, yet we "wait eagerly for our adoption . . . the redemption of our bodies" (v. 23). Survey the passage for other perspective shifts. Some of them will be treated in greater detail in subsequent questions.

Question 9. It's interesting to notice the condensation of time in this unique description of a Christian's stages in redemption. We think of God's calling and foreknowledge as past and of our glorification as future. Yet all appear here in the past tense. This reveals a sense of certainty (it is so certain that Paul speaks of it as having already occurred), but it also hints at the timelessness of God. We think of stages, with the most immediate one being where we are right now. God sees the big picture in such a complete way that he can speak of it as already past. God stands apart from time. If you need definitions of these highly complex theological terms, these simple explanations will do. Consider consulting a theological dictionary or commentary for more complete understanding. *Foreknow:* To have complete knowledge of; to know beforehand; also, have planned in advance. *Predestined:* Literally, determined in advance, appointed to a specific destiny. *Call:* Summons from God to bear the name of a Christian and to belong to God in Christ. *Justified:* God's forgiveness and treatment of sinners as if they had never sinned by substituting the crucifixion of Jesus as their punishment and crediting his sinlessness as their own. *Glorified:* The ultimate state of being completely perfect, conformed to the image of Jesus Christ. As you study these theologically packed verses, notice also the short explanation attached to each term in the biblical text. Notice also that each one leads inexorably to the next.

Questions 10-11. Verses 31-38 are so poetic that we can get lost in simply apprehending their beauty. Take a few moments to do that. Then take out a mental magnifying glass and examine the text for meaning. Start by marking the question marks. Then study the content and implications of each question. Tucked around the questions are a variety of objections or answers. Take all of this into account as you bring not only the beauty but also the meaning of this text into your own soul.

Question 12. This passage is permeated with the timelessness of God. This is true also of his love. It is an eternal love, not dependent on our current circumstances, limitations or pain.

Sources

The Wesley Family Tree
Rebecca Lamar Harmon, *Susanna: Mother of the Wesleys* (Nashville: Abingdon, 1968).

Study One
W. Reginald Ward (journal) and Richard P. Heitzenrater (manuscript journals and diaries), eds., *The Works of John Wesley,* vol. 18, *Journal and Diaries I (1735-38),* The Bicentennial Edition of the Works of John Wesley (Nashville: Abingdon, 1988), pp. 139, 141-43.

Study Two
Albert C. Outler, ed., *John Wesley* (New York: Oxford University Press, 1964), pp. 59, 66-67, 69.

Study Three
Thomas C. Oden, *The New Birth, John Wesley: A Modern English Edition* (San Francisco: Harper & Row, 1994), pp. 1-19.

Study Four
Outler, *John Wesley,* pp. 183-88.

Study Five
Charles Wallace Jr., ed., *Susanna Wesley: The Complete Writings* (New York: Oxford University Press, 1997), pp. 79-80, 83-84, 355-56.

Study Six
John Telford, ed., *The Letters of the Rev. John Wesley* (London: Epworth, 1931), pp. 304-6, 314, 319.

Further Reading

Baker, Frank, ed. *The Works of John Wesley*. Oxford: Oxford University Press, 1982.

————. *The Bicentennial Edition of the Works of John Wesley*. 27 vols. Nashville: Abingdon, 1984.

Bewes, Richard, comp. *John Wesley's England: A 19th Century Pictorial History Based on an 18th Century Journal*. New York: Seabury, 1981.

Green, J. Brazier. *John Wesley and William Law*. London: Epworth, 1945.

Harmon, Rebecca Lamar. *Susanna: Mother of the Wesleys*. Nashville: Abingdon, 1988.

Oden, Thomas C. *John Wesley's Scriptural Christianity: A Plain Exposition of His Teaching and Doctrine*. Grand Rapids, Mich.: Zondervan, 1994.

————. *The New Birth, John Wesley: A Modern English Edition*. San Francisco: Harper & Row, 1994.

Oden, Thomas C., and Leicester R. Longden, eds. *The Wesleyan Theological Heritage: Essays of Albert C. Outler*. Grand Rapids, Mich.: Zondervan, 1994.

Outler, Albert C., ed. *John Wesley*. New York: Oxford University Press, 1964.

————. ed. *The Works of John Wesley*. Nashville: Abingdon, 1985.

Pollock, John. *John Wesley*. Wheaton, Ill.: Harold Shaw, 1989, 1995.

Schmidt, Martin. *John Wesley: A Theological Biography*. Translated by Norman P. Goldhawk. New York: Epworth, 1962.

Telford, John, ed. *The Letters of the Rev. John Wesley*. London: Epworth, 1931.

Tuttle, Robert G. *John Wesley: His Life and Theology*. Grand Rapids, Mich.: Zondervan, 1978.

Wallace, Charles, Jr., ed. *Susanna Wesley: The Complete Writings*. New York: Oxford University Press, 1997.

Wesley, John. *The Works of John Wesley, Third Edition, Complete and Unabridged.* Edited by Thomas Jackson. 1831. Reprint, Grand Rapids, Mich.: Baker, 1996.

———. *Explanatory Notes upon the Old Testament.* Salem, Ohio: Schmul, 1975.

Wesley, John, and Charles Wesley. *Selected Prayers, Hymns, Journal Notes, Sermons, Letters and Treatises.* Edited by Frank Whaling, with a preface by Albert C. Outler. New York: Ramsey, 1981.